OUTHERN OCEAN

BY JUNIATA ROGERS

ANTARCTICA

SOUTHERN OCEAN

Published by The Child's World®
1980 Lookout Drive • Mankato, MN 56003-1705
800-599-READ • www.childsworld.com

Credits: Creative icon styles: 5, 14 (compass); demamiel62/Shutterstock.com:
6; Denis Burdin/Shutterstock.com: 21; Durk Talsma/Shutterstock.com: 10;
Iurii Kazakov/Shutterstock.com: 18; polarman/Shutterstock.com: 9; reisegraf.
ch/Shutterstock.com: 13, 17; wildestanimal/Shutterstock.com: cover, 1

ISBN HARDCOVER: 9781503825000
ISBN PAPERBACK: 9781622434374
LCCN: 2017960209

Printed in the United States of America
PA02373

TABLE OF CONTENTS

Where in the World? . . . 4

Small for an Ocean . . . 7

Summer and Winter . . . 8

Windy and Wavy . . . 11

A New Ocean . . . 12

Go with the Flow . . . 15

Too Cold? . . . 16

An Important Place . . . 20

Glossary . . . 22

To Find Out More . . . 23

Index and About the Author . . . 24

WHERE IN THE WORLD?

Where is the Southern Ocean? Look at the map. Find the Atlantic Ocean. Do you see it? What about the Pacific? The Indian? Look to the south. The oceans end in a straight line. The Southern Ocean starts there. It surrounds Antarctica.

The Southern Ocean is also called the Antarctic Ocean.

ARCTIC OCEAN

ASIA

NORTH
AMERICA

EUROPE

PACIFIC
OCEAN

ATLANTIC
OCEAN

AFRICA

PACIFIC
OCEAN

INDIAN
OCEAN

SOUTH
AMERICA

AUSTRALIA

The Southern Ocean is Earth's
second smallest ocean.

SOUTHERN
OCEAN

ANTARCTICA

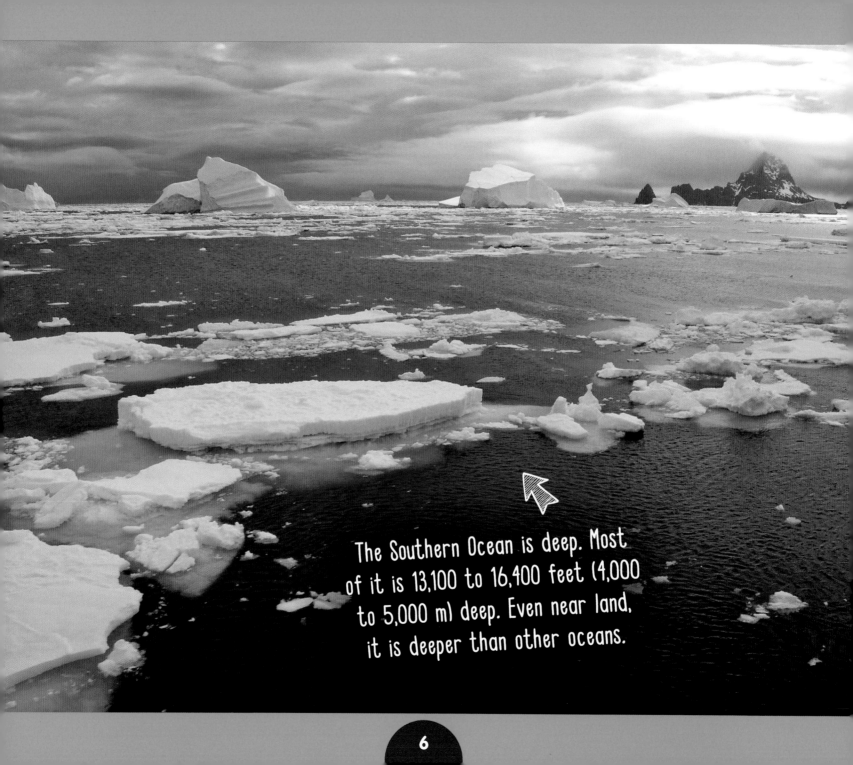

The Southern Ocean is deep. Most of it is 13,100 to 16,400 feet (4,000 to 5,000 m) deep. Even near land, it is deeper than other oceans.

SMALL FOR AN OCEAN

The Southern Ocean is small. It is the second smallest ocean. Only the Arctic Ocean is smaller. The Southern Ocean covers about 8 million square miles (20 million sq. km).

The Southern Ocean is about twice the size of the U.S.

SUMMER AND WINTER

The Southern Ocean is cold. In winter, ice covers it. Some of the ice melts in summer. But even in summer, the Southern Ocean is icy and cold.

There is six times more ice on the Southern Ocean in winter than in summer.

Ships must often break through the ice when sailing on the Southern Ocean.

WINDY AND WAVY

The Southern Ocean is windy! It has the fastest winds of any ocean on Earth. It has big waves. The weather is often stormy.

With very little land nearby to break against, waves on the Southern Ocean can be very large.

A NEW OCEAN

Today Earth has five oceans. Not long ago, there were four. In 2000, scientists named the Southern Ocean.

Before 2000, the Atlantic, Pacific, and Indian Oceans included the waters of the Southern Ocean.

Scientists study many different things about the Southern Ocean.

ARCTIC OCEAN

NORTH
AMERICA

EUROPE

ASIA

ATLANTIC
OCEAN

AFRICA

PACIFIC
OCEAN

PACIFIC
OCEAN

SOUTH
AMERICA

INDIAN
OCEAN

AUSTRALIA

The ACC is the only current
that circles Earth.

SOUTHERN
OCEAN

ANTARCTICA

GO WITH THE FLOW

The **Antarctic Circumpolar Current**

(ACC) flows around Antarctica. A current

is fast water that follows one path. The

ACC goes in a circle. It acts like a wall.

It keeps the Southern Ocean apart from

other water.

The ACC is also known as
the West Wind Drift.

TOO COLD?

Is the Southern Ocean too cold for animals? No! Squid and fish live here. Seals and whales do, too. **Plankton** and **krill** grow well here. That's important. Many other animals depend on them for food.

The colossal squid lives in the Southern Ocean. It can grow to be 46 feet (14 m) long.

Crabeater seals often rest on the ice in the Southern Ocean.

Adélie (uh-DAY-lee) penguins swim about 5 miles per hour (8 kph).

Penguins are the most well-known animal in the Antarctic. There are many different kinds! Gentoo, chinstrap, and emperor penguins all live, feed, and play in the Southern Ocean.

Leopard seals and orcas (killer whales) love to hunt penguins for food.

AN IMPORTANT PLACE

The Southern Ocean is Earth's coldest place. It is tough to visit! But we need the Southern Ocean. It brings life to the rest of the world.

The Southern Ocean's deepest point is the South Sandwich Trench. It is 23,740 feet (7,236 m) deep.

The Southern Ocean is sometimes called the South Polar Ocean.

GLOSSARY

Antarctic Circumpolar Current (ant-ARK-tik sir-kum-POHL-ur KUR-runt): The current that moves around the Southern Ocean. It circles the Earth around Antarctica.

krill (KRIL): Krill are very small shrimp-like animals. Many ocean creatures eat krill.

plankton (PLANK-tun): Plankton are tiny plants and animals that float through the ocean on currents. Many larger animals depend on plankton for food.

TO FIND OUT MORE

Books

Oachs, Emily Rose. *Southern Ocean*. Minneapolis, MN: Bellwether Media. 2016.

Spilsbury, Louise, and Richard Spilsbury. *Southern Ocean*. Chicago, IL: Heinemann Raintree, 2015.

Wilsdon, Christina. *Ultimate Oceanpedia: The Most Complete Ocean Reference Ever*. Washington, DC: National Geographic Children's Books, 2016.

Woodward, John. *Ocean: A Visual Encyclopedia*. New York, NY: DK Publishing, 2015.

Web Sites

Visit our Web site for links about the Southern Ocean:

childsworld.com/links

Note to Parents, Teachers, and Librarians: We routinely verify our Web links to make sure they are safe and active sites. So encourage your readers to check them out!

INDEX

animals, 16, 17, 18, 19
Antarctic Circumpolar Current, 14, 15
Antarctica, 4, 15
Arctic Ocean, 7
Atlantic Ocean, 4, 12

current, 14, 15

depth, 6, 20

ice, 8, 9
importance of, 20
Indian Ocean, 4,

krill, 16

leopard seals, 19
location, 4

other names, 4, 21
orcas, 19

Pacific Ocean, 4,
penguins, 18, 19
plankton, 16

scientists, 12, 13
size, 5, 7

South Polar Ocean, 21
South Sandwich Trench, 20
squid, 16
storms, 11

waves, 11
West Wind Drift, 15
winds, 10, 11

ABOUT THE AUTHOR

Juniata Rogers grew up in Newport, RI, an island town on the Atlantic Ocean. She has worked as a naturalist, an art model, and a teacher. She's been writing professionally for 25 years, and currently lives near Washington, DC.